Original title:
A House Made of Love

Copyright © 2025 Creative Arts Management OÜ
All rights reserved.

Author: Elliot Harrison
ISBN HARDBACK: 978-1-80587-146-0
ISBN PAPERBACK: 978-1-80587-616-8

Walls of Warmth

In the kitchen, laughter brews,
Spices dance with silly views.
Chairs that creak and giggles rise,
Flour on noses, sweet surprise.

The cat's a thief, stealing socks,
Jaywalking squirrels, silly knocks.
Cracks in the walls, tales unfold,
Each ding tells stories, funny and bold.

The Foundations of Affection

Foundation's strong, it's made of jokes,
Step on the floor, hear all the folks.
A little wobble, a playful bounce,
Watch out for the cat, she might pounce.

Windows wide for laughter's breeze,
Silly dance parties, all on knees.
Walls that shake with echoing mirth,
Creating joy, the essence of worth.

Heartstrings Entwined

In the living room, chaos reigns,
Pillow fights where no one gains.
A trampoline of loving care,
Who cares about the tangled hair?

Hugs that bounce, they seem to spin,
Tickles start, and giggles win.
With every moment, love's the thread,
Knitting warmth in every spread.

Embraced by Kindness

At the door, a welcome mat,
Oh, what fun to see the cat!
Dancing shoes all piled high,
Do the robot, oh my, oh my!

Every corner's filled with cheer,
Fill it up with snacks and beer.
Here's to friends, the foolish sort,
In this place, joy runs and cavorts.

Pillars of Connection

In the living room, laughter breaks,
Couch cushions thrown, oh what mistakes.
The dog sneezes, it's time to cheer,
Popcorn flies, let's bring on the beer.

In the kitchen, the chef is proud,
Spaghetti's flying — talk about loud!
Burnt toast here, and cookies galore,
All we need is love… and maybe a score.

Windows to the Heart

Our windows are cracked, that's no surprise,
They frame the sunsets, and some teary eyes.
Neighbors peek through, and we wave back,
   Holding a pie — wait, is that a snack?

Through these panes, the giggles ring,
As we dance with joy, to a silly swing.
Painted with laughter, framed with a grin,
These silly moments make us all win.

The Blueprint of Care

Sketches of hugs and a sprinkle of glee,
Blueprints laid out for you and me.
Naps on the floor, blanket forts too,
Who needs plans when we've got our crew?

Look at the layout, goofy and bright,
A wacky design that feels just right.
Even the cat has her cozy place,
Sleeping through chaos, with a meow and a grace.

Rooms of Radiance

In one room, the music plays loud,
Dancing like fools, we draw a crowd.
The chandelier sways, it's a merry sight,
As we twirl around, grace takes flight.

In another, games spark joyful fights,
Cards flying everywhere, oh what delights!
Laughter echoes from room to room,
Creating a rhythm that banishes gloom.

Cornerstones of Closeness

In a kitchen where laughter brews,
Spaghetti noodles dance in shoes.
A cat in a hat just walked the line,
Who knew such chaos could taste so fine?

In the living room, socks play hide and seek,
The dog wears a wig, oh so unique!
A pillow fight turns into a duel,
With giggles and grins as the main fuel.

On the porch, we sing off-key,
The neighbors join in, it's quite a spree.
Hot cocoa spills, and marshmallows fly,
Who knew joy could be so spry?

In the garden, weeds wear silly hats,
While gnomes engage in spirited chats.
We dance 'round the tulips in silly poses,
With love as our garden, anything grows.

Through the Keyhole of Trust

A hallway where secrets like to play,
Behind each door, laughter shouts hooray.
A broom with a mustache, oh what a sight,
Whirling and twirling in soft moonlight.

In the bathroom, bubbles take a stand,
Rubber ducks holding a rubber band.
A plunger in capes and masks they wear,
Saving the day with a goofy flair.

The attic's a treasure, a pirate's dream,
Toys come alive in a wild scheme.
Dust bunnies jig with a gleeful spin,
Who needs a crew when you've got kin?

We peek through the keyhole, oh what glee,
To find our hearts are the best curry.
Each room a tale of laughter and cheer,
With love spilling out, we're rich my dear!

Bricks of Belonging

Bricks made of giggles and laughter,
Wobbly walls that won't fall after.
Dodging chores with a playful grin,
Cuddles at dusk, where mischief begins.

Funky paint and quirky door,
Each room a tale to explore.
Socks on the ceiling, questions galore,
In this cozy chaos, who could ask for more?

Bound by Tenderness

Wobbling chairs and drowsy cats,
Snacks abound, we all sit like rats.
Tickle fights lead to silly snacks,
A chorus of love, with joyous clacks.

Whispers weave in the kitchen heat,
Funny stories in every seat.
From pancake flops to coffee spills,
In our clumsy dance, affection thrills.

Roof of Resilience

A roof that leans but never breaks,
With goofy games and delicious cakes.
Storms may knock, but we just laugh,
Under this cover, we find our path.

Umbrellas inside for unexpected rain,
With all these quirks, can we feel pain?
The thaw of winter brings jokes anew,
Our silly shelter just grew and grew.

The Sanctuary of Us

In our stronghold, the world's quite loud,
We dance like fools, all silly and proud.
Pillow forts that reach the sky,
With laughter echoing, oh me, oh my!

The sacred space where pets all scheme,
Whiskers twitch in a playful dream.
In this funny fortress, wild and free,
Love's our compass, just wait and see!

Foundations of Affection

In the basement of giggles, we lay our bricks,
With laughter so hearty, it brings in the kicks.
Each corner a quirk, with crumbs from our snacks,
Building this fortress, avoiding the cracks.

Jumps in the attic, where silliness reigns,
Ghosts of our pranks dance around in our brains.
Swing from the rafters, we shout with delight,
As love builds the walls, we'll party all night.

Embracing Every Corner

In every small nook, there's a tickle or tease,
Where socks disappear and the dust bunnies sneeze.
We paint the walls bright with our wild fantasies,
Our imaginations run like playful doggies.

Each room's a delight, a comedy show,
The cat thinks it's his; we just let him go.
With each silly dance, we've got rhythm and groove,
This house of our making makes it hard not to move.

Shelter of Solace

In the bathroom, we bubble, and splashes abound,
Rubber ducks dancing, our joy knows no bounds.
Cereal for dinner, we laugh in the kitchen,
While biscuits tumble down, we all start glitchin'.

The couch is a ship, and we sail on the sea,
With pillows as shields, we're as wild as can be.
Under blankets of laughter, we snuggle and roll,
In this kind of haven, we're free to be whole.

Love's Warm Embrace

Around the fireplace, we roast marshmallow dreams,
While sharing our stories, and silly memes.
The warmth of our banter fills up every crack,
We build it together, there's no looking back.

With socks on the floor and shoes tossed about,
Each moment a treasure, there's never a doubt.
In this silly abode, we make it our own,
Here in our chaos, a family is grown.

A Fortress of Faith

In a castle of socks, I guard my domain,
Where the wear and the tear are the source of my fame.
The walls made of laughter, the windows of cheer,
Who needs a moat when you have friends so near?

Cereal towers stand tall, breakfast's delight,
Spilled milk like a river, what a glorious sight!
With a shield of good humor, we battle each day,
In this fortress of joy, we'll laugh all the way.

Light in Every Corner

In the attic of giggles, where shadows gleam bright,
We turned off the lights, but we danced in the night.
With a flashlight for laughter and tickles galore,
Each corner a canvas, painted with more!

A sprinkle of chaos, a dash of good fun,
Where the dust bunnies play and the sun loves to run.
Illuminating moments with silly little quirks,
In this bright little space, laughter often lurks.

The Garden of Memories

In a plot filled with jokes, where the daisies all grin,
We planted our laughter, let the fun begin.
With weeds made of giggles and soil of delight,
Each bloom tells a story that's out of sight!

The broccoli chuckles, the carrots all sway,
In this garden of joy, come what may!
With friends as the gardeners, tending so true,
We harvest the smiles, and we share them with you.

Steps of Companionship

On the staircase of friendship, we trip with a grin,
Each tumble a memory, where laughter begins.
With each step a story, we dance and we lurch,
Creating a rhythm, a jubilant perch!

From the top to the bottom, we slide down with glee,
In this comedy show, there's always room for three.
Hand in hand, we leap, down the hall we explode,
In the steps of our journey, love's always bestowed.

A Bonded Sanctuary

In a castle built of giggles,
Where socks find their mismatched mates,
And the fridge hums funny tunes,
We dance on our own strange fates.

The curtains swing with wild abandon,
As the cat claims the sunny spot,
While the plants gossip in whispers,
And the kettle plays a hot-spot.

Bouncing ballads fill the air,
With backs against the wobbly chair,
We dodge the dust bunnies lurking,
In our lively love affair.

Chaos reigns in this sweet mess,
Where tasty snacks are shared with zest,
In every corner, joy is found,
Here, life is truly at its best.

Shadows of Serendipity

Shadow puppets dance at dusk,
The walls echo tales, long and husky,
We trip over life's silly pranks,
Yet our laughter's forever risky.

Mismatched mugs hold golden dreams,
In this quirky, cozy retreat,
We toast to the absurdity,
And always accept defeat.

Jumbled thoughts spill on the floor,
With snacks piled high by the door,
As the noise of love fills the air,
In shadows, we always explore.

Silly hats and fuzzy socks,
Family ties wrapped in knocks,
Here, every hour is a surprise,
In the warmth that never clocks.

Laughter Echoes Here

Echoes of laughter rise so sweet,
In every room, there's a happy beat,
Cookies shaped like alligators,
And puns that just can't be beat.

Whiskers twitch and kids collide,
With pillow forts as our only guide,
Who knew a spatula could be magic,
In a place where dreams abide?

Silly games and goofy dances,
Where everyone gets endless chances,
We twirl like leaves on a breezy day,
Chasing joy with wild glances.

Even the goldfish joins the fun,
Waving its fins like it's just begun,
In this lively hub, we gather 'round,
With hearts sparkling like the sun.

The Porch of Promise

On a porch that creaks with cheer,
We sip on lemonade, hold hearts near,
Where jokes tumble like falling leaves,
And every sigh's a happy tear.

The swing's a boat set to the moon,
While the nighttime stars sing a tune,
Whispers float on gentle breezes,
In this shelter, we dig our spoon.

With mismatched chairs and a lopsided view,
We share our secrets, old and new,
Crickets join in with their choir,
Creating a symphony for a few.

Every sunset paints our dreams,
In this cozy spot, life redeems,
With love as strong as grandma's stew,
Every moment's worth it, or so it seems.

Light Filtering Through Love

Sunlight dances on the floor,
Tickling toes with warmth galore.
Laughter echoes off the walls,
Joy spills out as chaos calls.

Cupcakes melt on kitchen shelves,
Sticky fingers, elves and elves.
Giggling fits in every nook,
Where even dust bunnies cook.

The Canvas of Us

Crayons spill, a rainbow bright,
Masterpieces in the night.
Splatters here and smudges there,
Artistic mess without a care.

Each brushstroke tells a tale,
Of silly fights and ice cream trails.
Walls adorned with winks and grins,
Where laughter starts and never ends.

Rooms Filled with Joy

Pillow forts rise high and proud,
Echoing giggles, oh so loud.
Toys in corners, chaos blooms,
In cozy land, there's always room.

Tickle monsters roam the halls,
Stealing socks and chuckling calls.
In every room, a dance unfolds,
As stories swap and laughter holds.

Creating Comfort in Chaos

Laundry piles that touch the sky,
An obstacle course to fly.
Cooking with a splash of flair,
Mismatched socks dance without care.

Finding peace in every mess,
With hugs that soothe and laughter bless.
In this whirlwind, love will grow,
Even when we steal the show.

A Tapestry of Togetherness

In our quirky castle, cats roam free,
We dodge the dust bunnies, just you and me.
Pizza boxes piled, like towers of dreams,
With laughter echoing, bursting at the seams.

Socks on the ceiling, laundry's a game,
We draw our own map, but who's to blame?
Every spilled drink is a toast to the fun,
In this wild tapestry, we've barely begun.

The Fire of Unity

Our kitchen's a circus, with pots clanging loud,
We dance through the chaos, we're lost in the crowd.
Burnt toast is the norm, gourmet not required,
We laugh through the smoke, our spirits inspired.

When dinner is over, the dishes are stacked,
A tower of memories, somehow intact.
Together we shine, though our skills are a mess,
In this fire of unity, we're truly blessed.

Love's Architectural Dream

We built walls of giggles, a roof made of grins,
Our flooring's a dance floor, where clumsiness wins.
Each brick laid with jokes and a sprinkle of cheer,
A structure so silly, it wobbles our fears.

Blueprints of chaos, we draft with delight,
Every room's a riddle, surprise and a fright.
In this whimsical dwelling, we're never alone,
For together we thrive, a kingdom we've grown.

Paths of Passion

Our garden's a mishmash, weeds waltzing in line,
With daisies and dandelions, all intertwined.
We trip over laughter, each corner a jest,
In this wobbly maze, we feel truly blessed.

Chasing the sunshine, we skip through the raindrops,
Collecting our memories, we keep them in Stops.
With each silly stumble, our hearts beat anew,
On these twisting paths, love's wild and it's true.

Kindness' Cornerstone

In the kitchen, cookies fly,
Sugar rushes, oh my, oh my!
Mommy's giggles, flour on her nose,
Dancing round the chef, how sweet it grows.

Silly socks upon the floor,
Every corner hides a roar.
A dog who thinks he's quite the cat,
Chasing shadows, imagine that!

Board games stacked, yet none can play,
All too busy, come what may.
Whispers linger, laughter sounds,
In this chaos, love abounds.

Chairs that wobble, tables creak,
Family feuds can make you weak.
Yet every squabble lifts our cheer,
In the end, we'll always steer.

Heartfelt Halls

Walls painted bright, with quirks galore,
Memories hang like notes of lore.
A family portrait, someone forgot,
Pajama parties, oh, what a plot!

Sneaky snacks behind the chair,
Finding treasure everywhere.
Socks and shoes in every space,
Love's a dance, a silly race.

The hallway echoes with silly songs,
As we all parade, it won't be long.
Each step a giggle, each turn a twist,
In a world of smiles, how can you resist?

Stairs that creak with every jump,
Falling down makes for the best thump.
In these hearty halls, joy expands,
When life confuses, we hold hands.

Threads of Togetherness

Yarn and laughter twist and knot,
Crafting memories — give it a shot!
Hide and seek behind the drapes,
A tickle here for giggly shapes.

Art supplies all over the place,
Who drew that? Oh, what a face!
Toys in piles, a race to find,
Masterpieces made by kids combined.

Dining table, a color spree,
Spaghetti stains and a cup of tea.
Siblings bicker, but only for fun,
Together we shine like the rising sun.

Time to play, so set the scene,
A treasure hunt, the prize is green.
In this mess, true joy is spun,
Together we laugh, and we've already won.

Where Hearts Converge

In the living room where chaos thrives,
An old cat sleeps, while the dog dives.
Neighbors pop in with pies and cheer,
"Who let the cat out?" rings sincere!

Bookshelves wobble, stories stacked,
Every corner filled, love intact.
Lost the remote? Don't shed a tear,
In this circus, it disappears.

Outdoor picnics, ants in line,
Sandwiches shared, everyone fine.
Laughter echoes on this green stage,
In this playground, we engage.

When all is done, and day turns dark,
We settle in, share one last spark.
In this lively place, we shall always merge,
Where every heart finds the urge.

Harmony's Hearth

In the kitchen, spills and laughs,
Pasta fights and butter gaffs.
Mom's secret spice, a wink and grin,
Dad burns toast, yet still we win.

With socks as pets, we dance and twirl,
A game of hide-and-seek unfurl.
The dog steals dinner, who's to blame?
In chaos' weave, we find our fame.

The Essence of Togetherness

We build a fort with sheets and chairs,
The cat gets lost, but no one cares.
Popcorn fights and movie night,
Remote control, our laughter's flight.

In silly hats, we sing off-key,
A family band, just you and me.
Chasing shadows till we fall,
In this whirlwind, we have it all.

Nest of Nurture

Our garden grows with jokes and puns,
And weeds that tickle as we run.
With each flower, a secret shared,
In muddy boots, our hearts are bared.

Rainy days with games galore,
Socks become boats on kitchen floor.
With giggles echoing through the air,
In our little world, love is rare.

Making Memories Canvas

With crayons big, we draw our dreams,
In wiggle-squiggles, nothing seems.
Every doodle, a cherished tale,
In our art, we shall prevail.

Scrambled eggs on dad's new shirt,
Tickle fights that really hurt.
In every mess, a joy to find,
Together, always intertwined.

Open Doors to Tenderness

Open doors swing wide,
The puppy dashes in,
Furniture's on the ceiling,
Where do we begin?

Laughter echoes softly,
Cooking's gone awry,
Spaghetti on the cat,
Bouncing here and there, oh my!

Socks are mismatched treasures,
Dancing on the floor,
We'll find the lost remote,
In the fridge? What's in store?

Tickles turn to giggles,
Hugs that feel like pies,
In this quirky haven,
Love's the best surprise!

Windows to the Soul

Windows wide and gleaming,
Birds peek in to chat,
Calico cat is scheming,
With plans to chase that brat.

The garden's full of chatter,
Bees buzz a happy tune,
Flowers dress in laughter,
Their colors make us swoon.

Sunshine spills in golden,
Where pancakes fly and flip,
Every meal's a story,
With a side of funny quips.

With teamwork on the table,
Dishes dance and sway,
Windows watch us giggle,
As we bloom in our way!

Nourished by Kindness

Warm croissants are laughing,
Butter melts like gold,
Coffee spills like secrets,
In this joy-filled hold.

The blender joins the party,
It sings a silly song,
Fruit parades in colors,
Big and bold, not wrong!

Hearts are always cooking,
With a sprinkle of cheer,
Every bite is cozy,
When kindness draws us near.

Plates piled high with humor,
Laughter fuels the taste,
In this sweet communion,
We savor joy, no waste!

The Spine of Togetherness

In this place of bumbles,
A spine of warm delight,
We stand in silly poses,
Ready for a sight!

Jumping on the sofa,
Dance parties break out loud,
Socks fly like confetti,
We're a rambunctious crowd!

Board games turn to battles,
With giggles never cease,
We cheer for every blunder,
Where fun will find its peace.

The spine, it bends with laughter,
In a twist of pure glee,
Together we are stronger,
In this wild jubilee!

The Verse of Our Shelter

In a place where socks go missing,
And the cat insists on kissing.
We throw pillows into the air,
As laughter bounces everywhere.

The fridge is full but never neat,
Leftovers hiding, a smelly treat.
We dance in the kitchen to silly tunes,
Between the pasta and wooden spoons.

The bathroom's jammed with too much stuff,
Yet all we need is a little fluff.
With rubber ducks and bubble baths,
We find joy in our silly paths.

Our walls may creak, our floors may squeak,
But joy is found in every peek.
With every door that swings and clacks,
Home is where the fun never lacks.

The Essence of Together

In our space of mismatched chairs,
Love is found in silly stares.
With tickle fights and silly games,
We forget each other's names.

The laundry piles up—who's to blame?
Is it the dog or the cat to tame?
We play hide-and-seek in plain sight,
As the world's worries slip from our sight.

Beneath the shelves of stacked-up books,
We share secrets and silly looks.
With pizza sauce on every plate,
We giggle until we're far too late.

Every corner holds a funny tale,
With happy hiccups that never pale.
In this space, our hearts collide,
With giggles and joy as our guide.

Whispers in the Walls

The walls conspiring, they seem to grin,
With secrets and jokes woven in.
Each creak narrates a funny fate,
As we argue 'bout who's running late.

The ceiling laughs when we jump high,
As dreams float up into the sky.
Jokes ricochet like bouncing balls,
Echoing laughter through the halls.

In each corner, mischief resides,
With little messes our love provides.
The dust bunnies dance under the bed,
While stories of silliness can be read.

In our humble abode of quirk and glee,
We find joy in the chaos, just you and me.
With every whisper, the walls reveal,
That love can be strange, but oh so real.

Heartstrings Entwined

With mismatched socks and random hats,
We create a symphony—just us rats.
Silly dances in the living room,
As we twirl away the impending doom.

Our spoons and forks do a crazy jig,
While the dog tries to be a big gig.
Sneaking snacks after dark's the game,
While stealthy giggles ignite the flame.

We stack the cushions, reach the sky,
Pretending we're pilots soaring high.
Counting every star from the porch,
Where laughter flickers like a torch.

Though days can be chaotic, it's true,
Together we chase skies of blue.
In every twist, our hearts blend fine,
With fun and love, our hearts entwine.

Pillars of Passion

In a kitchen where pancakes do fly,
With syrup rivers, oh me, oh my!
The coffee pot sings, in a cheerful hum,
While socks on the ceiling bring giggles to some.

The living room's dance floor is set each night,
With disco balls made of fairy light.
Don't mind the cat, he thinks he's the star,
As we two-step to tunes from the old car.

In the den, we craft stories, quite bizarre,
Of dragons that beat up a chocolate bar.
With laughter echoing off every wall,
Our joy turns each fumble into a ball.

The hallways are filled with mismatched shoes,
And secrets whispered to the morning news.
In this silly space where we all belong,
Our hearts beat in rhythms of a joyful song.

Nestled in Togetherness

With the couches so cozy, we squash side by side,
A remote control battle, with snacks as our guide.
We're pillow fort builders with plans that are grand,
And popcorn explosions meet every demand.

The front door's a portal to worlds quite absurd,
Where mailmen deliver confetti, not word.
With rainbows of socks tossed all over the floor,
We laugh as they tell tales of days gone before.

Together we wander the aisles of our dreams,
With lists that include all sorts of silly schemes.
From discovering how jump ropes made us sweat,
To dancing with brooms, our funniest pet.

In a realm of chaos where joy's always near,
Our hearts simply dance, and there's nothing to fear.
We'll sip on hot cocoa, both messy and sweet,
As we share secret glances that make life complete.

Garden of Gentle Moments

In our tiny garden, weeds wear silly hats,
As we plant seeds of laughter amidst chubby rats.
With shovels as swords, we duel over dirt,
Claiming our kingdom with mud-caked shirts.

The flowers sing softly, a tune quite absurd,
As butterflies giggle and dance with a bird.
Our watering can sprinkles its joy like a show,
While worms wiggle wildly, putting on quite a glow.

Sunsets provide us a canvas for fun,
Where we draw silly faces, each one a home run.
In the warmth of our garden, we find peace and play,
As mother nature chuckles the whole livelong day.

So here in our patch, where whimsy takes root,
We sow seeds of joy, like a big, silly fruit.
With gentle moments, we're rich beyond measure,
In this garden of giggles, we harvest pure pleasure.

Love-Concealed Spaces

In our closet of secrets, old hats hold tales,
Of adventures that ended with giggles and wails.
When the vacuum's a monster, we plan a retreat,
With blankets for armor, we laugh at our feat.

Every nook is a treasure, each cranny a smile,
The attic holds memories that stretch for a mile.
With dust bunnies plotting a takeover at night,
We whisper sweet dreams under blankets of light.

Behind every curtain, a new giggle awaits,
As shadows play tricks with our plush teddy mates.
We craft stories of pirates on journeys so bold,
In our love-concealed spaces, where magic unfolds.

So here in our castle made funky and fun,
With each silly moment, we bask in the sun.
For joy is our language, and laughter the key,
In our quirky little world, just you, me, and glee.

Walls That Listen

In a room where secrets dwell,
The walls gossip, can't you tell?
They chuckle softly, laugh out loud,
Holding stories, oh so proud.

They hear the jokes, all well-timed,
And sometimes wonder if they're rhymed.
With every whisper, every shout,
They're the best friends, without a doubt.

As dishes clatter, and kids collide,
The walls just grin, they take it in stride.
Who knew bricks could have such fun?
In this house, laughter's never done!

So come on in, join the spree,
These walls can hold such clarity.
In every crack and every seam,
They keep our joy; it's quite the dream!

Kindred Spirits Abode

In a cozy nook with quirky flair,
We dance like no one's even there.
With socks that mismatch, and smiles so wide,
It's pure delight, it's our joyride.

The ceiling drips with laughter, true,
While hippos serve tea in shades of blue.
With friends who snort, and laugh so loud,
We twirl like dervishes, feeling proud.

We've got a pet rock who sings off-key,
He's the life of the party, can't you see?
This home's a circus, with love as glue,
A splendid mix of silly, too!

So come on over, don't be shy,
We assure you, there's a reason why.
In this warm den, we share our cheer,
Where kindred spirits gather near!

Sanctuary of Shared Dreams

In realms where dreams play hide and seek,
Our visions twirl, our futures sneak.
We share the giggles of secret plans,
And make peace treaties with rubber bands.

With pillow forts that scrape the sky,
And late-night snacks as we sit near by.
The weirder, the better, it's just our way,
Who knew daydreams could lead to play?

Dance parties start at half-past eight,
In our sanctuary, we celebrate fate.
With disco balls that shine so bright,
Our dreams take flight in the moonlight.

A tad too loud? Oh, perhaps we are,
But every heart's a shining star.
In this space, where wishes gleam,
We weave our stories—a shared dream!

The Hearth of Harmony

In the center of our quirky lair,
Sits a hearth that keeps us in flair.
It crackles tunes, it hums along,
With marshmallow dreams and laughter strong.

Gather 'round, bring stories to tell,
The fire's warm glow casts a spell.
With every marshmallow, toast it right,
Our harmony dancing, a joyful sight.

Let's roast our worries, one by one,
And savor the warmth of everyone.
With chilly nights and hearts aglow,
Our hearth's the place where love can grow.

So bring your quirks, your laughter, too,
This is a space where we're all anew.
With humor and heart, we'll never stray,
In our hearth of joy, forever we'll play!

Emotions Engraved

In the kitchen, laughter brews,
Cooking chaos, with silly cues.
Spaghetti dances on the floor,
Meatballs roll, we shout for more.

In the hallway, secrets creep,
Whispers light, as shadows leap.
Tickle fights beneath the stairs,
Giggles echo, filling airs.

On the couch, we trip and fall,
Pillow fights become a brawl.
Chasing dreams 'neath blankets warm,
Every jump, a quirky charm.

From the garden, fruit trees sway,
Juicy fun in bright array.
This life we build, with glee and gaff,
Emotions etched, a hearty laugh.

The Spirit Within

In the attic, dust motes twirl,
Forgotten toys and a magic girl.
Her dolls chat with such delight,
Holding court in the evening light.

Downstairs, the TV's always loud,
Family cheers, we're one big crowd.
Commercials pause for jokes so bad,
And wonder why they call us mad.

In the basement, treasures await,
Board games stacked in splendid state.
Each rolled die and every card
Turns our night into something hard.

Yet through walls that seem to bend,
Our joy remains, it won't end.
In every nook, a giggle sings,
The spirit's dance, in playful rings.

Calming The Storms

When thunder roars and clouds start to cry,
We build a fort, just you and I.
Pillow walls to shield the fright,
With snacks galore, we'll win this fight.

As raindrops tap on window panes,
We play pretend, ignore the pains.
Superheroes rescuing from fear,
With laughter loud, we dry each tear.

The oven hums a sweet warm tune,
Cookies rise to fill the room.
With sprinkles tossed like shooting stars,
We'll bake our dreams, ignore the scars.

Through storms we dance, we sing, we shout,
No need for umbrellas, there's joy about.
In the storm's heart, we find our calm,
With silly faces and cookie balm.

Embraces in Every Room

In the living room, hugs abound,
Silly faces spin around.
Each embrace, a gentle tug,
Squeezing tight, like a warm mug.

The dining room, where food spills wide,
Messy joys, we just can't hide.
The sauce that splats, the crumbs that fly,
With every bite, we laugh and sigh.

In the bathroom, rubber ducks float,
Singing songs, they seem to gloat.
Bubbles rise like giggling chimes,
As we wash away our times.

Each room's a stage, with love's own flair,
Cozy chaos fills the air.
In every corner, a chuckle blooms,
Embraces thrive in all our rooms.

Echoes of Devotion

In the halls where laughter reigns,
Even the walls have shared some gains.
The fridge hums songs of midnight snacks,
While shoes lie strewn, like playful hacks.

The chairs gossip when no one's around,
Whispers of love, not meant to astound.
Socks with holes tell tales of mishaps,
As echoes of joy create funny gaps.

Every nook has a quirky tale,
Of spilled drinks and a rattling snail.
The ceiling fans twirl in mock delight,
As shadows dance in the soft moonlight.

With every step, the floorboards squeak,
A symphony of joy, so to speak.
In a space where chaos becomes the art,
You'll find the rhythm of a happy heart.

The Heart's Blueprint

Blueprints scribbled on a napkin,
Dreams of a kitchen meant for snacking.
With pots that giggle when they're too hot,
And a toaster that sings when it's not.

The couch, a throne for lazy kings,
Holds court with crumbs and random things.
Keyboards clicked with love's sweet tunes,
While dust bunnies dance to silly tunes.

Walls adorned with mismatched art,
Each piece a memory, a funky part.
From framed selfies to cat portraits,
Every glance tells joy that waits.

In the corners, a laundry pile sprawls,
A mountain of clothes, where laughter calls.
For every bump and bruise we bear,
A home becomes love, beyond compare.

Harmonies Beneath the Roof

Beneath this roof, melodies play,
From morning coffee to the end of day.
The kettle whistles a high-pitched tune,
While socks on the line hope to fly soon.

Plates that clink, a ballet so fine,
As forks and knives do a sassy line.
In the cabernet haze of a Saturday night,
The curtains sway with a soft delight.

The vacuum croons in rhythmic delight,
Chasing down crumbs that scale new heights.
And when the cat darts across the floor,
Harmony shrieks as laughter soars.

So gather round, let the music swell,
In this quirky place, we all dwell.
For love is the tune that we can't mute,
In a chaos of joy, we take our root.

Love-Laden Beams

The beams above seem to conspire,
Holding secrets of love in a funny mire.
Each creak they make is a chuckle shared,
As memories dance, unprepared.

Stools that wobble with tales untold,
Of game nights lost and snacks too bold.
Pillows thrown in laughter's fight,
As giggles erupt in the depth of night.

Light fixtures flicker like fireflies bright,
Sharing silly puns drenched in light.
They twinkle down at the mishaps below,
A spotlight on life's comedic show.

And when the day gives way to dreams,
This playful chaos bursts at the seams.
A quirky love wrapped in beams so tight,
Creating a home where all feels right.

Emblems of Endearment

In a fortress of giggles, we thrive,
With socks on the ceiling, oh, how we strive.
A dog in the laundry, a cat on the chair,
Our memories stacked up like old teddy bears.

From pasta to pizza, our feasts are a riot,
Mixing up flavors? It feels like a diet!
With dance-offs at midnight and puns at the door,
It's chaos, but who could ever want more?

Love notes on napkins, they greet us each day,
With doodles and hearts that never decay.
A kitchen of mischief, a hallway of cheer,
This merry abode, where laughter is near.

So here's to our haven, both silly and sweet,
With mismatched decor, it's perfect, complete.
In this quirky retreat where the fun doesn't cease,
We build our own world, our joyful release.

Twilit Talks

Under the stars, we hatch our grand schemes,
With pillows for partners, we plot and we dream.
A blanket fort kingdom, where shadows all dance,
We trade midnight secrets and silly romance.

With cookies and milk, we giggle away,
Whispering stories that always did sway.
The floor might be cluttered, the ceiling's no prize,
But in our snug bubble, the laughter just flies.

Our antics might baffle the folks next door,
As we blast our tunes and then dance on the floor.
The night holds our secrets, our painted delight,
In this realm of our making, the future feels bright.

So let's raise a toast to the whims that we share,
To tongue-in-cheek love and our jumbled affair.
With twilit talks echoing, hearts all ablaze,
We find there's true magic in these silly ways.

Love's Timeless Design

In this space made of chaos, we laugh and we play,
With jigsaw puzzles scattered, they brighten our day.
A sofa that's seen more than a few playful spills,
But love's got a formula, that's full of good thrills.

With quirky old paintings hung upside-down,
We wear our weirdness like the finest crown.
A charm bracelet jingling with stories to tell,
It's a comedy club, and we're under its spell.

The floors might be messy, the fridge sings a tune,
While we keep our lives in this humorous boon.
A recipe's brewing, a dash and a splash,
Our dish might explode, and we all break out in laughs.

Here's to our dwelling, a whirlwind of glee,
To the memories crafted in highs and in spree.
With every odd moment, our hearts intertwine,
In this priceless design, our love can't confine.

Elements of Emotion

In the heart of our playground, we frolic and roam,
Where socks sprout legs, and play-dough feels like home.
Our laughter reverberates, it spins and it twirls,
Through every wild corner, our imaginations swirl.

The laundry may grumble with clothes on the floor,
But let's face it, dear friend, who could ask for more?
With breakfast for dinner and carrots that dance,
We savor the oddities, each whimsy's a chance.

From matchbox car races to pillow fights wild,
Here joy reigns supreme, even when we're exiled.
An oven afire with our latest dessert,
We're concocting sweet stories while playfully flirt.

So gather up laughter and sprinkle it wide,
In this tapestry woven with mischief and pride.
Emotions are plenty in this refuge we claim,
Our quirky abode will forever stay the same.

Beneath the Eaves of Connection

Under the roof where giggles play,
We chase the dust bunnies all day.
Mom's secret stash of cookies hides,
While dad pretends he never chides.

Laughter echoes through the halls,
As kittens chase after all the falls.
Silly hats and goofy shoes,
In our home, we never lose.

The walls may creak, the windows rattle,
But inside these rooms, we love to prattle.
Game nights spent in boisterous cheer,
We dance around with no sense of fear.

So here's to the joy that we all share,
Building our dreams with tender care.
Beneath this roof, we come alive,
In this quirky place where we all thrive.

The Attic of Affection

In the attic, dust clouds swirl,
Where old toys and memories unfurl.
Ghosts of laughter, a playful crew,
Whispering secrets, just us two.

Among the cobwebs, we play hide and seek,
Finding treasures unique and cheek.
A bicycle with a rusty bell,
Echoes adventures we know too well.

Old photos scattered like scattered dreams,
Painted faces with silly themes.
Each snapshot tells a laughable tale,
Of the times we would trip and fail.

Up in the attic, we stash our delight,
Turning drab days to sheer delight.
Among the mementos, love's worth is clear,
In this magical place, there's nothing to fear.

Where Memories Gather

In the corner, a chair so worn,
Where tales of past have been reborn.
The cushions squish with every laugh,
While we recount our crazy path.

Around the table where stories flow,
We spill our hearts and let them glow.
With every meal served with a hug,
We find old spoons that fit just snug.

Under the stairs, a treasure chest,
Filled with goofy things we love best.
Outfits from Halloween's worst fright,
We line them up for fun-filled nights.

This gathering spot, where love ignites,
We dance like fools under starry nights.
In this corner, we always cling,
To memories that make our hearts sing.

Colors of Companionship

In our home, the hues are bright,
With crayons scattered, what a sight!
We paint our walls with laughter's glow,
As rainbows dance in joyful show.

Socks mismatched in every drawer,
A colorful life that we adore.
Splashes of paint on every door,
Tell tales of fun and so much more.

Chasing each other through the halls,
Where giggles bounce off painted walls.
Each color holds a story true,
Like wacky hats and our antics too.

Companionship sewn in each stitch,
In a quilt of love, we find our niche.
With every shade, our hearts align,
In this cheerful home, we forever shine.

Shelter of the Soul

Under the roof of giggles and grins,
Silly debates and where fun begins.
We dance in the kitchen, step on toes,
In this crazy place, everyone knows.

Joking about socks that never match,
With playful pranks, we always hatch.
The dog steals a shoe, we give chase,
In our zany spot, we find our place.

When the rain falls, we race inside,
Finding new games, nowhere to hide.
Board games scattered around the floor,
In laughter's arms, we ask for more.

So bring your quirks and funny hats,
In this cozy nook, we're all just chats.
A shelter made from warm heartbeats,
Where joy is served in generous heaps.

Where Laughter Grows

In a garden of giggles, we plant the seeds,
Where ticklish jokes bloom like wild weeds.
Silly faces drawn on the wall,
Every corner whispers, come one, come all.

Dancing with shadows, we twirl and sway,
Chasing the sunlight, in our own way.
The cat wearing slippers feels so grand,
In our laughter field, life's always planned.

Socks on the ceiling and pizza for lunch,
We gather together, there's never a crunch.
With knock-knock jokes, we gather round,
In our joyful patch, happiness found.

So water it well with love and glee,
This garden of laughter, come plant with me.
Together we'll grow in the sun's soft light,
In a whimsical space, everything feels right.

Hearth of Togetherness

In the heart of the home where silliness reigns,
We gather for snacks and silly refrains.
Making the most of each playful wink,
Sharing our secrets over a drink.

The couch is a ship on the ocean vast,
With pillows as sails, we're anchored fast.
We argue about pirates and who's the best,
In this cozy kingdom, we're all jest-rested.

With hot cocoa mustaches and marshmallows galore,
We make a big mess, but we always want more.
Riddles and rhymes are our nightly bliss,
In our hearth's embrace, we find joy in this.

So let's light the fire, keep the laughter near,
Here bathed in warmth, we hold each dear.
With every chuckle and heartened cheer,
Our gathering spot is the best place, I fear!

Echoes of Embrace

In the echoes of laughter, our spirits unite,
Silly stories emerge under soft, twinkling light.
With quirks and odd jokes that make us snort,
This goofy finale is our favorite sport.

Slippery floors make a wildcard dance,
Ending up giggling as we take the chance.
A surprise tickle when someone sits down,
In our theatre of joy, no time for a frown.

We cuddle like blankets, cozy and tight,
Creating sweet memories, fueling delight.
With noodle-throwing duels in the dining room,
Every burst of laughter dispels any gloom.

So gather around for a moment of bliss,
In echoes of embrace, there's nothing amiss.
Our quirky troupe thrives, happy and bold,
In this vibrant space, where stories are told.

Strength in Sweetness

In the kitchen, flour flies,
While we share our goofy sighs.
Sugar spills like laughter loud,
Baking treats for all the crowd.

Jars of jam, a sticky mess,
But it's our kind of happiness.
Whisking dreams with fervent cheer,
Sweetness grows when you are near.

Frosting faces, a playful fight,
Giggles echo through the night.
Candy hearts, a silly craze,
Love's a game, a joyful maze.

In our cozy, crazy space,
Every blunder found a place.
Strength in sweetness, laughter loud,
Here's our joy, forever proud.

Ties That Bind

Silly socks that never match,
Hiding treasures, what a catch!
In the laundry, colors clash,
Tangled threads in wild mustache.

Dinner plans that go awry,
Pasta sticks, oh me, oh my!
But we laugh 'til we can't breathe,
Love's the bond that we weave.

Board games turn to comedy,
As we bicker joyfully.
With a wink, a playful shove,
These are ties we know and love.

Every silly, silly fight,
Brings us closer, feels just right.
Life's a dance, a game we find,
With laughter here, our hearts entwined.

Cherished Moments Here

Coffee spills and toast that burns,
Morning giggles, patience turns.
In the chaos, love ignites,
Cherished moments, pure delights.

Dancing socks on kitchen floors,
Burst of laughter, open doors.
Cartwheels down the hallway's length,
With each tumble, love's our strength.

Tales of dragons, socks that hide,
In this world, we laugh with pride.
Every twist, a story spun,
Memories made, forever fun.

When we gather, voices blend,
In our hearts, the joy won't end.
Each small moment, something dear,
A treasure chest, our laughter here.

Whims of Warmth

Wacky hats and mittens too,
Funny faces coming through.
Snowball fights and wild snowmen,
Warmth and giggles, once again.

Outdoors splash, puddles rise,
Rubber boots, a sweet surprise.
Silly dances with a glee,
Wet and wild, just you and me.

Evenings spent in cozy throws,
Watching movies, silly shows.
Popcorn flies like joy in flight,
Laughter echoes through the night.

In the warmth of shared delight,
Every whim, a pure delight.
Together in our playful spark,
Lights our love, a glowing arc.

Shades of Comfort

In the corner, a cat takes a nap,
While the dog plots the next treat caper.
The sofa's a throne for the snacks we share,
And cushions serve as our cozy paper.

We dance on the floor with mismatched socks,
Spinning 'round like a whirlwind spree.
Each laugh turns the walls into joyful stage,
Where our quirks become a sweet symphony.

The fridge hums a tune only we know,
It keeps secrets in leftovers and ice.
Each shelf holds a story, bizarre yet true,
Our humble abode, a slice of paradise.

When the doorbell rings, we hold our breath,
Who's crashed our party today, oh my!
It's the neighbor with cookies, or just odd socks,
Either way, we share a hearty laugh and pie!

The Melody of Home

In the kitchen, pots and pans collide,
As the dog joins in with a happy bark.
The microwave beeps a curious tune,
While sibling rivalries light up the dark.

Oh, the floor creaks as we race to the hall,
Who can't resist this silly game?
Lost socks are the treasures we can't find,
And laughter is our binding flame.

With each goofy dance in the living room,
We create the rhythm of our shared space.
Our family ties are each silly move,
Together we draw a priceless grace.

Under blankets, we plot our next prank,
Pillow fights are our highlights of the day.
Every giggle echoes off loving walls,
In this melody, we forever play.

Chambers of Joy

Enter the hallway of ticklish feet,
Where echoes of laughter are freshly baked.
Our family room's a comedic show,
With silly poses and snacks we make.

In the nook, a treasure of games piled high,
We battle with laughs and a tickle fight.
And every defeat is met with a grin,
Because winning is fun, but joy is our light.

The pets rule the roost, it seems very clear,
Their antics add flair to our sweet abode.
As we gather 'round for a movie night,
Whiskers in popcorn should never unload.

We close our eyes to just catch a wink,
Yet dreams are filled with moments so bright.
Who knew such chambers could hold such delight,
In every little giggle, our love takes flight!

Floors that Feel

Tiptoe on floors that squeak and sway,
Each creak is a note in our song's display.
With mismatched shoes, we prance and flip,
Every room's a stage for our joyful trip.

In the dining room, it's a feast of fun,
Spaghetti fights 'til the set is done.
A sauce splash here, a cheese wheel roll,
Each meal a laugh, that's how we roll.

The bathroom's a stage for our best puppet shows,
With rubber ducks watching the antics grow.
Every corner tells a tale, my dear,
Laced with giggles and no sign of fear.

At the end of the day, as we settle down,
Our hearts, with laughter, wear a crown.
With floors that feel like our playful song,
We know together is where we belong.

A Tapestry of Together

In a room where socks collide,
And mismatched mugs reside,
Laughter echoes off the walls,
Where silly dance moves enthrall.

The fridge hums a quirky tune,
As leftovers loom like a cartoon,
Tickling our senses with spicy old peas,
While the cat performs daredevil trees.

Puzzles gather dust in the corner,
As we jest like jovial mourners,
Our wild ideas sparking delight,
Even when the dog steals a bite!

Every nook tells a funny tale,
Like when the cake went stale,
In this lively, jumbled space,
Joy flourishes with its funny face.

Love's Foundation Stone

Amongst the clutter, we assert,
A pile of laundry and a smelly shirt,
As we argue over who takes out the trash,
There's always a giggle that makes the day flash.

The kitchen's a battleground of yum,
Where burnt toast pops like a drum,
Wobbling cakes like dancing fools,
Fill the air with the best of our drools.

Coffee cups with doodles galore,
Silly notes stuck to the door,
Love brewed strong in this daily grind,
In our chaos, we joyfully unwind.

With every silly spat and jest,
We weave a life that feels so blessed,
In this merry mess, so perfectly flawed,
A blueprint for joy—well-loved and awed.

Beneath the Canopy of Care

Beneath the roof where giggles reign,
And every joke comes with a stain,
We twirl in a living room tango,
Dodging the cat's wild, playful fandango.

In the garden, weeds grow like friends,
While we argue where the hose ends,
The clouds above gossip and tease,
As raindrops dribble off the trees.

Mismatched chairs at our dining table,
Each a story, a laugh, a fable,
Over meals that sometimes combust,
It's always love, laughter, and a crush.

Every corner brims with delight,
A rollercoaster ride through day and night,
Wrapped in blunders our hearts hold dear,
In this cherished chaos, all we need is near.

Touchstones of Affection

In a realm where shoes lose their pairs,
And secret snacks hide under chairs,
We giggle like kids when we trip and fall,
Our home's like a circus — we just give it our all!

The laughter bubbles up like a stew,
When one of us cracks a joke out of blue,
Each moment a gem, shiny and bright,
As we wrestle pillows in a silly fight.

The bathroom's a stage for our morning routine,
With toothpaste fights and hair gel sheen,
Our antics light up the everyday grind,
Creating memories, the best you can find.

In this playful chaos, love dances and sways,
It's the glue that binds all our ways,
Amongst all the quirks and blunders we share,
Our bond grows stronger, woven with care.

www.ingramcontent.com/pod-product-compliance
Lightning Source LLC
Chambersburg PA
CBHW060131230426
43661CB00003B/383